BAT HOSPITAL

Clare Hibbert

PowerKiDS
press.

New York

Published in 2015 by
The Rosen Publishing Group, Inc.
29 East 21st Street, New York, NY 10010

Library of Congress Cataloging-in-Publication Data

Hibbert, Clare, 1970- author.
 Bat hospital / Clare Hibbert.
    pages cm. — (Save the animals)
 Includes bibliographical references and index.
 ISBN 978-1-4777-5886-1 (pbk.)
 ISBN 978-1-4777-5881-6 (6 pack)
 ISBN 978-1-4777-5888-5 (library binding)
 1. Tolga Bat Hospital—Juvenile literature. 2.
Bats—Diseases—Australia—Juvenile literature. 3.
Bats—Conservation—Australia—Juvenile literature.
4. Tick-borne diseases in animals—Australia—
Juvenile literature. 5. Veterinary medicine—Juvenile
literature.
I. Title.
 QL737.C5H53 2015
 599.4—dc23
                                 2014026400

Copyright © 2015 by
The Rosen Publishing Group, Inc.

First published in 2015 by Franklin Watts
Copyright © Arcturus Holdings Limited

Editor: Joe Harris
Picture researcher: Clare Hibbert
Designer: Tokiko Morishima

Picture credits: all images Eric Baccega/Nature PL
except pages 2–3: Pete Oxford/Nature PL and pages
5 (bg) and 14-15 (bg): Shutterstock. Cover image:
Pete Oxford/Nature PL

Manufactured in the United States of America

CPSIA Compliance Information: Batch #CW15PK: For Further Information contact
Rosen Publishing, New York, New York at 1-800-237-9932

CONTENTS

TOLGA BAT HOSPITAL

In a remote part of Queensland, Australia, is a very special hospital — Tolga Bat Hospital. It is named after the **Tolga Scrub**, the area of rainforest where it is found. Its patients are sick, injured, or orphaned flying foxes.

The Tolga Scrub is an important habitat for flying foxes, also known as fruit bats. These amazing animals are the largest kind of bat in the world. They have big eyes and doglike faces. Spectacled flying foxes roost in the canopy (the highest branches) in the Tolga Scrub. There are also black flying foxes and little red flying foxes.

Bats roost in the flight cage at Tolga Bat Hospital.

Tolga

AUSTRALIA   Tolga Bat
Hospital

Jenny Maclean set up the Tolga Bat Hospital in 1997. She bought a five-acre (two-hectare) area of the forest and began to grow native plants on the land to help conserve it. She still runs the hospital and is passionate about saving bats and protecting Australian wildlife. At first, her hospital worked only with flying foxes. Today it looks after many different kinds of bat.

TROUBLE WITH TICKS

In the mid-1980s, large numbers of spectacled flying foxes began dying mysteriously. Dozens of dead and dying animals were found on the forest floor. Scientists warned that spectacled flying foxes were a threatened species, at risk of extinction.

It was not until 1990 that two researchers, Bruce and Ann Johnson, discovered the cause of the problem. All of the dead and dying bats had been bitten by paralysis ticks. "Paralysis" means not being able to move, and the bites were making the bats unable to open and close their feet, so they could not roost.

Fact File: Ticks

Ticks are parasites that live by sucking blood. They go through different life stages. Before each change, paralysis ticks feed on an animal's blood. Some animals, such as koalas, are immune to (not hurt by) the poisons in their bite. Flying foxes are not immune.

As more rainforest has been cut down to make way for farms, buildings, and roads, there has been less food for the bats. When they leave the forest looking for food, they come into contact with the ticks. Then they carry them back to their colonies.

TICK TREATMENT

If they are found and treated in time, bats that have been bitten by paralysis ticks can recover. The hospital workers search the colony twice a day for affected bats. They take the bats back to the hospital for treatment.

The first job is to find the tick and pinch it off the bat's body. It's important not to leave any of the tick's mouthparts behind – this could cause an infection. The caretakers check whether the bat can be saved, or whether it would be kinder to put it to sleep. If the patient is a mother bat, her pup is usually taken away to be cared for separately.

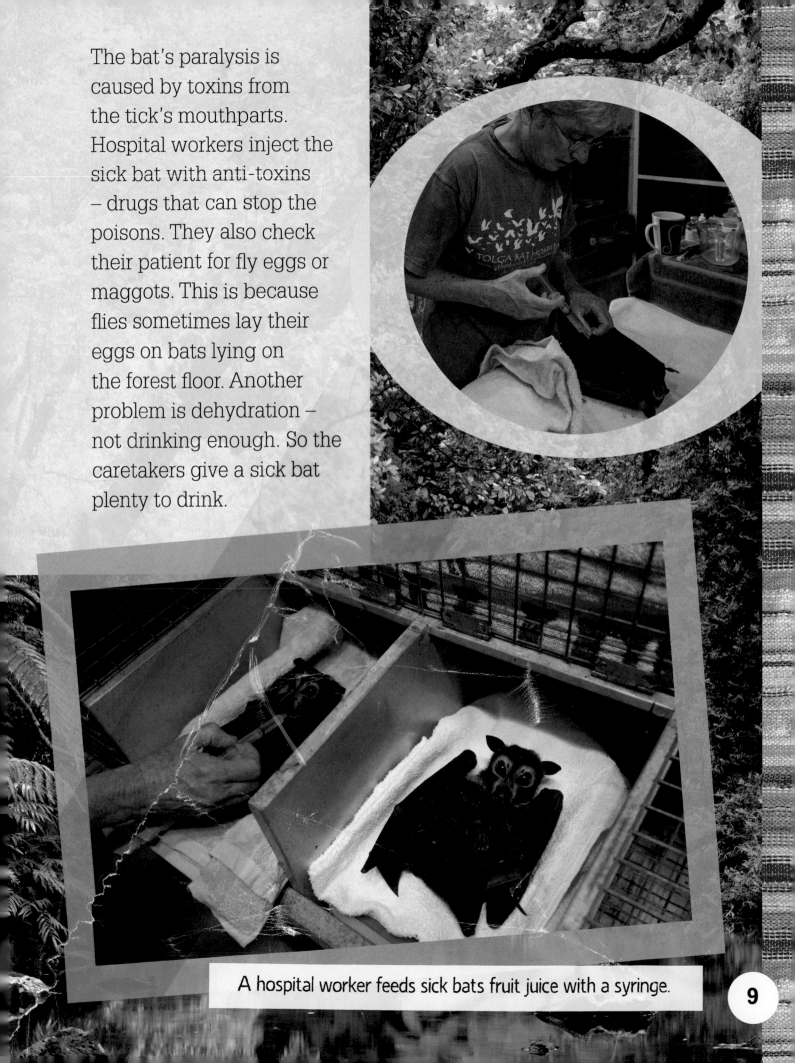

The bat's paralysis is caused by toxins from the tick's mouthparts. Hospital workers inject the sick bat with anti-toxins – drugs that can stop the poisons. They also check their patient for fly eggs or maggots. This is because flies sometimes lay their eggs on bats lying on the forest floor. Another problem is dehydration – not drinking enough. So the caretakers give a sick bat plenty to drink.

A hospital worker feeds sick bats fruit juice with a syringe.

THE NURSERY

Baby bats are used to being tucked safely under their mother's wings. At Tolga, the caretakers wrap the orphans in little blankets called swaddling cloths. It keeps them warm and stops them from hurting themselves or each other with their clawed wings and feet.

Until they are eight weeks old, the orphans are fed only on milk. Just like human newborns, they must eat every two to four hours. The pups are given human baby formula or powdered cows' milk with added glucodin, a sugar that is easy to digest.

Fact File: Bat Babies

A spectacled flying fox's pregnancy lasts seven months. She gives birth to a single pup between October and December. That time of year is spring in Australia, so there should be plenty of food for the mother to eat while her body is making milk.

Older babies take their milk through rubber teats from babies' bottles. Sometimes they even sleep with a teat in their mouth! It seems to comfort them. Newborns are too tiny to feed from the rubber teats. Instead, caretakers drip milk into their mouths using a syringe. It takes a long time!

HOSPITAL WORKERS

Almost all of the staff at the hospital are volunteers. Some are students or travellers who stay at Tolga for a few weeks or months. They work for no pay but they all agree that the volunteering is very rewarding.

The hospital has one full-time member on staff and around 10 volunteers who live locally. In addition, about 35 other volunteers stay each year from around the world. Most come during the tick season, from October to February, which is also when spectacled flying foxes have their babies. This is the hospital's busiest time. The volunteers live on site in tents. It means there are people to care for the bats around the clock.

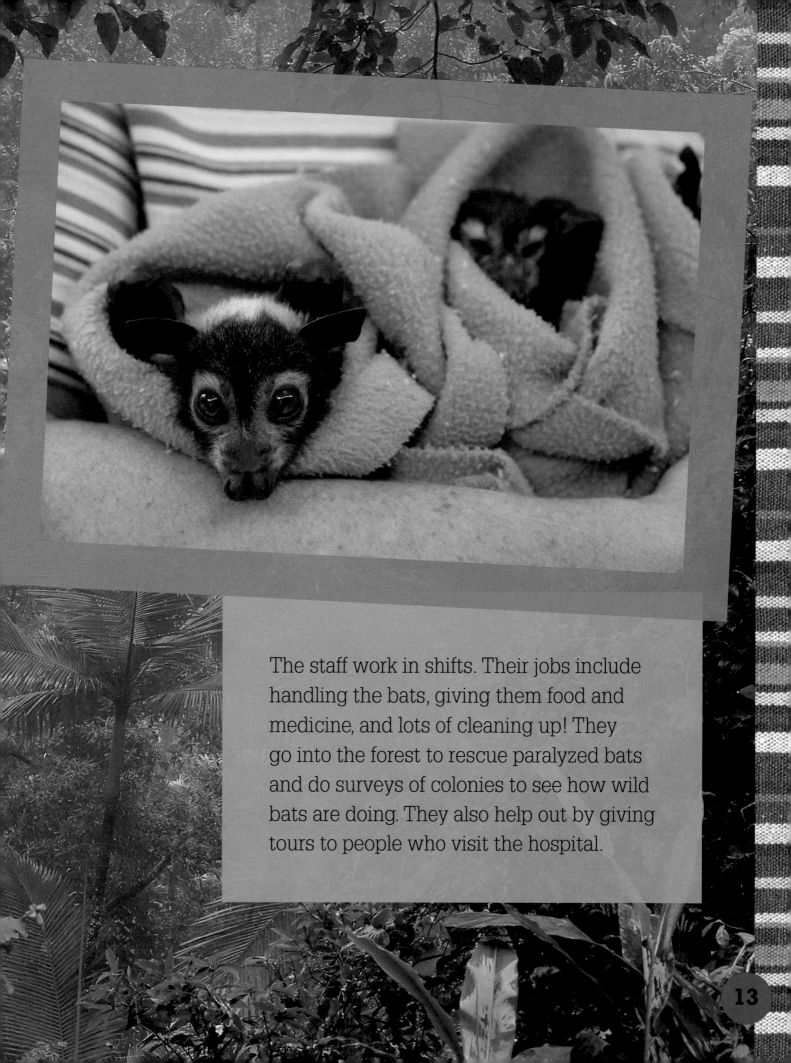

The staff work in shifts. Their jobs include handling the bats, giving them food and medicine, and lots of cleaning up! They go into the forest to rescue paralyzed bats and do surveys of colonies to see how wild bats are doing. They also help out by giving tours to people who visit the hospital.

HEALTH CHECK

Every bat that is brought into the hospital is given a thorough health check. Volunteers keep careful notes of their findings so they can track how each patient is doing. They quickly learn to recognize the individual bats!

The bats are weighed regularly so the hospital staff can check that they are putting on weight at the right rate. This is especially important for babies as they are still growing and developing. Swaddling makes the bats easy to weigh because they don't flap around on the scales.

A volunteer checks an orphan's microchip number.

The volunteers also keep notes on the bats' other measurements as they grow, such as their wingspan and their body length. Caretakers do everything calmly and quietly with no sudden movements. They check the animals' heartbeats for signs of stress.

Fact File: Microchipping

The hospital microchips each bat. A tiny computer chip, the size of a grain of rice, is put under the animal's skin. Each chip has a unique number. If it's found again in the future, the bat can be identified and matched back to its medical records.

PREPARING MEALS

Flying foxes feed on fruit, flowers, and sweet, honeyed nectar. In the wild, they spend all their waking hours finding food and feeding. At Tolga, the volunteers spend most of their day preparing fruit for the bats!

Most of a wild flying fox's diet is made up of tropical fruits, such as figs and guavas. Trucks arrive at Tolga laden with crates of fruit, which all need to be unloaded and stored. Volunteers chop up the fruit. Watermelons, for example, have a tough outer skin that the bats cannot bite through. Some days, more than 175 pounds (80 kg) of fruit are prepared.

A volunteer carries strings of apples.

The volunteers stick chunks of fruit onto wires to hang from the bats' cages. Harder fruits, such as apples, take more effort to eat – especially if they're threaded on long wires or S-shaped hooks. "Working" for their food keeps the bats from getting bored. Bananas are another favorite. Some are simply peeled and placed inside wire mesh feeders. Others are saved for blending up into smoothies – delicious!

DINNERTIME!

The volunteers make sure there is food available to the bats all the time. As well as putting out fruit, they hang up leaves from mulberry and fiddlewood trees. The green leaves are full of important vitamins that the bats cannot get from fruit.

The little red flying foxes at the hospital feed mainly on nectar and pollen so the volunteers put out flowers for them. White tea tree blossom is a favorite with the bats. The hospital also has tube-nosed bats. They are fruit feeders but they can be fussy – some will only take fruit juice!

Bats are famous for echolocation – finding food in the dark using sound. Only small bats do this, however. Flying foxes rely on sight and sound to locate their food. Volunteers often hide the food in the cages. This encourages the bats to move more, speeding up their recovery.

Fact File: Bat Diets

Not all bats eat fruit. Fishing bats skim over lakes and rivers, catching fish to eat. Other species feed on frogs or on other bats and some even suck blood! Most small bat species are insectivores (they eat only insects). A pipistrelle bat can eat more than 3,000 insects a night!

THE FLIGHT CAGE

The bat orphans begin their stay at hospital in the nursery. When they get stronger, they are moved to the flight cage. There is enough space for the bats to stretch their wings and practice flying.

Some bats in the flight cage are still too injured to fly. Even so, being in the cage helps them to grow stronger by climbing and moving around. It's like an adventure playground for bats, large enough to include trees, ropes and nets! The trees give them some shade, but there are sunny areas where the flying foxes can bask, fanning themselves with their wings.

When they are resting, bats hang upside down. This means their wings are always ready for takeoff. In the wild, they grip the bark of a tree. At the hospital, they hold on to the mesh of the cage. Their legs and feet are designed so that the bat's body weight keeps the toe claws gripping tightly, even when the bat is asleep.

FOSTER CARE

In a typical season, Tolga Bat Hospital rescues about 300 orphaned bats. It doesn't have the space, staff or money to look after all of these. Around two-thirds are cared for elsewhere.

When they are bigger, stronger, and nearly ready for release back into the rainforest, the fostered orphans come back to Tolga. They are transported by air in crates with mesh tops that they can grip. Each crate is divided into individual roosts, so the bats cannot claw each other.

When the bats arrive back at the hospital, the first thing the volunteers do is give them a drink. Travelling is a thirsty business! Each bat is given a health check. Once they have had time to recover from the journey, they can begin the process of returning to the wild.

TOLGA BAT HOSPITAL
ATHERTON. QLD. 4883
07 4091 2683

LIVE BATS
B 4
B 5
B 6

TOLGA BAT HOSPITAL
ATHERTON QLD 4883
07 4091 2683

LIVE BATS
C 6
C 5
C 4

TOLGA BAT HOSPITAL
ATHERTON, QLD 4883
07 4091 2683.

Fact File: Hospital Costs
Food — for both the bats and the volunteers — is the hospital's biggest expense. There are microchips and doses of antitoxin to buy, vets' bills to pay and general running costs. The hospital relies a lot on grants and donations. It also raises money through its visitor center.

RETURN TO THE WILD

A few of the bats at the hospital are too injured to ever return to the wild. They will stay at the center their whole lives. For most, though, the aim is to go back to the rainforest colony. It is a slow process.

The first stage is to move the bats to the release cage, which is in the middle of the forest near wild mothers and babies. At first, the cage is kept shut while the bats get used to the new sights, smells, and sounds. After a few days, the volunteers open the cage door. This allows the bats to rejoin their wild cousins.

The release cage

Even after the cage is opened, the bats come back to it for food. Learning about life in the colony is tiring and they are not used to finding their own meals yet. They need to build up their strength to fly longer distances. Volunteers put fruit in the cage for about five months. All this support gives the bats the best possible chance of surviving in the wild.

DANGERS TO BATS

At first, Jenny and the team at Tolga worked only with spectacled flying foxes that were suffering the effects of paralysis ticks. But before long they were helping other bats in need. Bats face many dangers in the wild.

Some bats go to the hospital after being caught on barbed wire or power lines. Others are found tangled up in the netting that protects farmers' crops and may have gone days without food. As long as they are found in time, the bats can be nursed back to health.

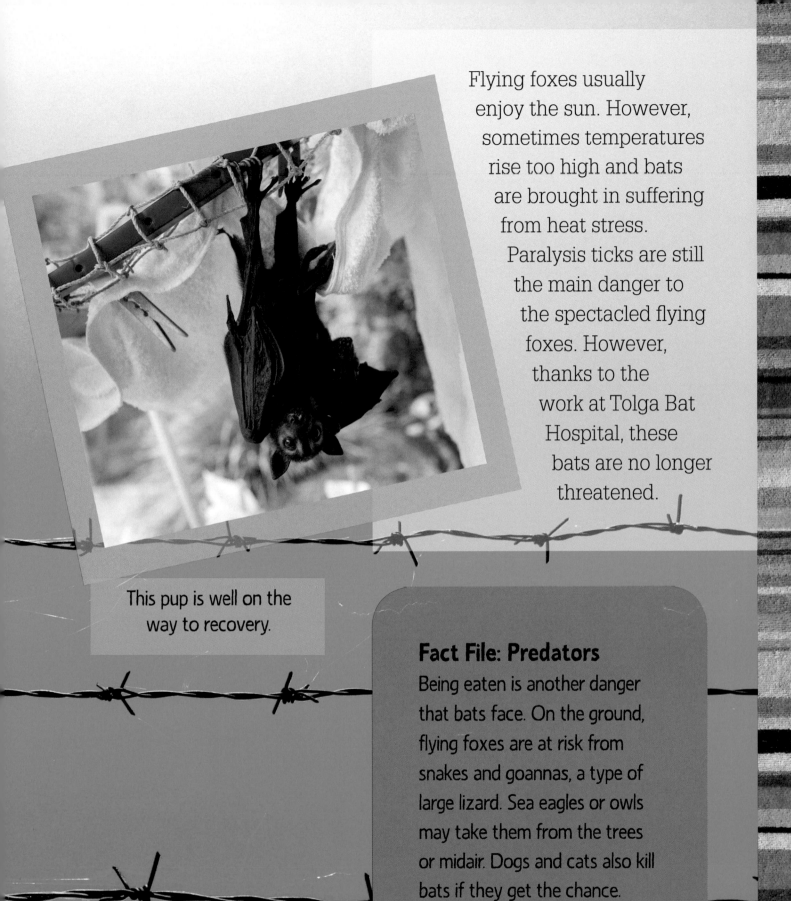

Flying foxes usually enjoy the sun. However, sometimes temperatures rise too high and bats are brought in suffering from heat stress. Paralysis ticks are still the main danger to the spectacled flying foxes. However, thanks to the work at Tolga Bat Hospital, these bats are no longer threatened.

This pup is well on the way to recovery.

Fact File: Predators

Being eaten is another danger that bats face. On the ground, flying foxes are at risk from snakes and goannas, a type of large lizard. Sea eagles or owls may take them from the trees or midair. Dogs and cats also kill bats if they get the chance.

REACHING OUT

As well as saving bats' lives, Tolga Bat Hospital works to teach people more about these animals. It shows people how important it is to conserve the bats' rainforest habitat. Thanks to Jenny and her team, the bats have a brighter future.

At the visitor center, people learn about bats and the threats to them firsthand. Some people are afraid of flying foxes or think of them as pests because they strip trees of fruit and leaves. Seeing the bats up close helps people see how vulnerable they are. The center raises much-needed funds for the hospital by charging visitors an entrance fee and selling souvenirs in its shop.

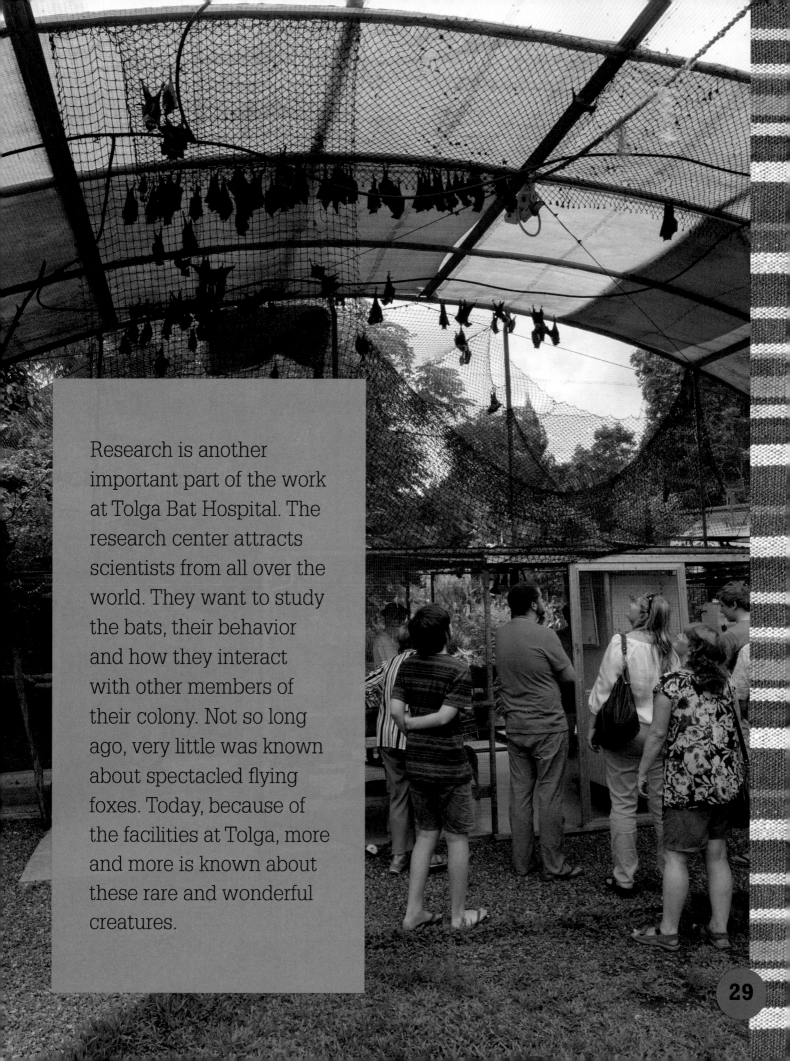

Research is another important part of the work at Tolga Bat Hospital. The research center attracts scientists from all over the world. They want to study the bats, their behavior and how they interact with other members of their colony. Not so long ago, very little was known about spectacled flying foxes. Today, because of the facilities at Tolga, more and more is known about these rare and wonderful creatures.

29

GLOSSARY

CANOPY The uppermost layer of rainforest vegetation (plant life).

COLONY A group of animals of the same species that live closely together.

CONSERVE To protect and keep for the future.

DEHYDRATION Lacking fluids.

ECHOLOCATION Detecting an object's location by producing a sound and then sensing how the echoes bounce back.

EXTINCTION Disappearing forever.

FOSTERED Brought up or cared for by someone else.

GRANT Money awarded for a special purpose, for example by a government or a charity.

HABITAT The place where an animal or plant lives.

IMMUNE Safe from a particular danger.

INFECTION A disease or condition caused by germs such as bacteria.

INTERACT Behave with one another.

NATIVE Naturally found in a place.

NECTAR A sweet liquid produced by flowers to attract animals such as bats and bees.

ORPHANED Having lost its parents. In bat society, where only mothers raise the pups, a baby that has lost its mother counts as "orphaned."

PARASITE An animal or plant that survives by living off another animal or plant.

PREDATOR An animal that survives by hunting, killing, and eating other animals.

RAINFOREST A thick tropical forest where there is heavy rainfall.

SHIFT The time that a person works.

SWADDLING Wrapping in a blanket.

THREATENED Describes a species of animal on its way to becoming endangered (at risk of dying out completely) in the future.

TICK A bloodsucking parasite belonging to the arachnid family, related to spiders.

VOLUNTEER Someone who works for free. Volunteers at Tonga are not paid but some receive free lodging and food in return for their work.

VULNERABLE Weak and at risk.

ZOOLOGY The scientific study of animals.

FURTHER INFORMATION

FURTHER READING

100 Facts: Nocturnal Animals by Camilla de la Bedoyere (Miles Kelly Publishing, 2010)

Animal Neighbours: Bat by Stephen Savage (Wayland, 2007)

The Bat Scientists by Mary Kay Carson (Houghton Mifflin Harcourt, 2010)

Endangered Animals of Australia by Marie Allgor (PowerKids Press, 2011)

Eyewitness: Jungle (Dorling Kindersley, 2009)

Eyewonder: Rainforest by Helen Sharman (Dorling Kindersley, 2004)

WEBSITES

Due to the changing nature of Internet links, PowerKids Press has developed an online list of websites related to the subject of this book. This site is updated regularly. Please use this link to access the list:

www.powerkidslinks.com/sta/bat

INDEX

SAINTS OF THE SOUTHWEST

SAINTS OF THE SOUTHWEST

BY JIM GRIFFITH

RIO NUEVO PUBLISHERS
TUCSON, ARIZONA

Rio Nuevo Publishers
an imprint of
Treasure Chest Books
P.O. Box 5250
Tucson, Az 85703-0250
(520) 623-9558

FIRST EDITION

ISBN 0-9700750-1-4

Editor: Ronald J. Foreman
Design: Larry Lindahl,
Lindahl-Bryant Studio, Sedona, AZ

Printed in Korea

10 9 8 7 6 5 4 3 2

FRONT COVER: *San José in the west
transept of Mission San Xavier del Bac
near Tucson, Arizona.*

PAGE ii: *Private chapel of Eulogio and
Zoraida Ortega in Velarde, New Mexico.*

CONTENTS

INTRODUCTION

SAINTS WERE ONCE REAL PEOPLE just like us—or rather the sort of people many of us strive to be like at least some of the time. What sets the saints apart from the rest of us is the complete and unswerving devotion with which they served God in this life. So great was their faith and so selfless were their acts of charity that—at the moment of death—each was ushered directly into the presence of the Lord.

From their exalted, heavenly home, the saints continue to demonstrate their concern for the welfare of humanity. They *care* and will help us whenever and however they can, if we humble ourselves and appeal to them in prayer. Saints cannot perform miracles; only God can do that. But saints can serve as effective intermediaries and advocates—lawyers, if you will—presenting the needs and hopes of earnest petitioners before the Most High.

That's the official, ecclesiastical view of saints. But in the popular mind, things can get a bit blurred. Many folks believe that the saints can and will act on their own accord, especially if the matter doesn't require a true miracle. Thus, believers appeal directly to Saint Anthony (San Antonio) to help find lost objects; to Saint Raymond (San Ramón) to be present during a difficult childbirth; and to Saint Isadore (San Ysidro) to bring rain. Specific requests are directed to specific saints, based on the personal interests and responsibilities that each saint demonstrated in life.

The life stories of most of the saints are known, and wonderful stories they are. Some are actually based on history and have been well documented, while others are more allegorical. In fact, there are saints about whom we really know nothing except their names. Saints Barbara and Christopher are among these and were in fact removed from the official Roman Catholic calendar in the 1960s, when the church determined that it had insufficient evidence about these individuals to justify their inclusion.

That certainly hasn't stopped ordinary people from praying to them. Saint Barbara is still popularly recognized as the patron of artillerymen, and travelers still reassure themselves by wearing Saint Christopher medals.

A cada santo su día—to every saint his day, so the Spanish proverb says. Indeed, the church officially honors recognized saints by marking dates on the religious calendar when specific individuals are to be celebrated. Formally, each celebration takes the form of a special Mass. In traditional Hispanic communities, saints' days can be marked with fiestas, involving lots of food, music, and ritual dancing. The annual pilgrimage to Chimayó, New Mexico, during Holy Week typically draws tens of thousands, as does the October San Francisco fiesta in Magdalena, Sonora, a few miles south of the Arizona border. More often,

Nuestra Señora de Guadalupe carved by Juan Pedro Espinosa Reyna in the yard of his cousin, Anibel Reyna, in Oquitoa, Sonora.

these fiestas are family or community affairs. In all cases, they are times in which one can say "thank you" to—and renew one's ties with—a favorite saint.

There are literally hundreds of saints. This book is devoted to thirty who are most popular among people residing in the border states of the United States and Mexico. We purposely chose to feature saints who are especially well known and loved throughout the region, as well as saints who are particularly popular in specific communities. Our search for images of these saints led us through Arizona, New Mexico, and the western tip of Texas, and across the border into the Mexican states of Sonora and Chihuahua.

Not all the individuals included in this book are saints in the strictest sense of the term. Neither the Christ Child—manifest here as the Holy Child of Atocha—nor the three important angels are saints, per se. We chose to include these figures here because, in the devotional life of the faithful, they are revered in much the same way as the saints themselves. Among the saints, the Virgin Mary—in all of her various manifestations—is distinguished from the rest by virtue of her role as the mother of God.

From the outset, we wanted to find images of saints who are involved in the daily devotional lives of ordinary folks. The representations featured in this book were not created as secular works of art to be housed in museums or galleries. Most of them occupy sacred places in churches, chapels, private homes, and roadside shrines.

These figures certainly are not idols. Rather, they serve to remind the faithful of sacred narratives and enable people to focus their thoughts and prayers.

Finally, our intent with this book is neither to promote nor to proselytize. Rather, we want to encourage readers, regardless of spiritual tradition, to gain a greater understanding of, and appreciation for, this fundamental aspect of our wonderfully rich and complex Southwestern culture. ✢

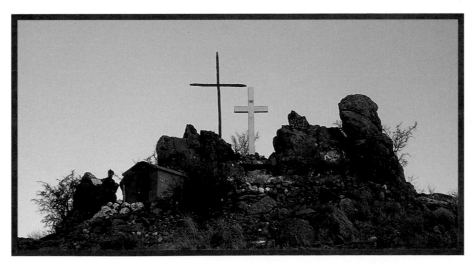

Hilltop shrine to Nuestra Señora de Guadalupe near Casas Grandes, Chihuahua.

THE
HOLY CHILD
OF
ATOCHA

✛ THE HOLY CHILD OF ATOCHA is a special manifestation of the Christ Child. This devotion seems to have originated in the Mexican silver mining town of Plateros, Zacatecas, when a statue of the Christ Child, which had been attached to the image of Our Lady of Atocha, got separated from His mother and took on a life of His own. Despite this apparent New World origin, a popular legend states that the Child of Atocha was accustomed to bringing food to prisoners in Spain. During World War II, He was the patron of the New Mexico National Guard imprisoned at Bataan in the Philippines.

El Santo Niño de Atocha usually is shown dressed in blue, with a cockleshell on His collar. This, along with His staff, water gourd, and floppy hat, mark Him as a pilgrim on the Way of Santiago de Compostela. He also carries a basket of food, and sometimes a set of shackles. He is the patron of prisoners and miners, but also assists anyone needing help, perhaps little boys especially. People visiting His statue often leave tiny pairs of shoes with Him because He is believed to wear out many pairs on His errands of mercy around the countryside.

Here's a story I was told a few years ago in Santa Ana Viejo, Sonora. Sometime in the 1980s, a little boy wandered away from his parents while they were stopped beside the highway between Santa Ana and Hermosillo, Sonora. When he didn't return, searchers were sent out. After more than a day of looking through the hot desert country, people had just about given up hope when the little boy appeared— fresh, rested, and healthy. He said that he had been scared at first, but then another little Boy appeared with a gourd of water and a basket of food. The two played together for a while and had a picnic lunch, and then the stranger Boy led His new friend out to the road and safety.

OPPOSITE: *El Santa Niño de Atocha in His shrine in the Santuario at Chimayó, New Mexico.*

RIGHT: *Mural painted by Antanasio Lajeno in the chapel of the old jail in Cananea, Sonora.*

1

SAN MIGUEL ARCÁNGEL

✝ THE LEADER OF THE HEAVENLY HOST, Saint Michael is the personal enemy of, and victor over, Satan. For this reason he also escorts souls to heaven, and will assist in the Final Judgment. Because the Devil traditionally is believed to occupy the middle air, churches to Saint Michael have been built on many mountain-tops, including Mont-San-Michel off the coast of Normandy. As Henry Adams said in the first sentence of his wonderful book *Mont-San-Michel and Chartres*, "The Archangel loved heights." His day, often called Michaelmas Day in English, is September 29.

San Miguel's predilection for heights is undiminished. He usually is clad as a Roman soldier—winged, sword in one hand and scales in the other, and poised over the supine body of Satan or a dragon. The scales are a specific reference to the last Judgment, when San Miguel will weigh the souls of the dead. He is also the patron of bankers, grocers, radiologists, and paratroopers, and is invoked against peril at sea.

THE ARCHANGEL MICHAEL

No wonder he was in the minds and hearts of Christians who ventured into new lands, which for all they knew were physically occupied by the Devil and his minions. Just as it is still Mexican and Hispanic custom to erect a cross on dangerous hilltops and shoot guns into the air at fiestas to drive Satan away, so San Miguel, in image or in name alone, guards many a perilous high place in the border states.

OPPOSITE: *This painting of San Miguel vanquishing his adversary was done by New Mexico santero J.D. Martínez, Jr., and is part of the altar in the chapel of Manny Gurulé outside Santa Fe, New Mexico. Here Satan takes the form of a serpent, which the saint is spearing while preparing to strike it with his sword.*

LEFT: *This graceful eighteenth century Mexican statue stands in the central niche of the main altar of the San Miguel chapel in Santa Fe, New Mexico. This chapel, the oldest church in Santa Fe, was built in the early seventeenth century, burned down in the Pueblo Revolt of 1680, and rebuilt between 1693 and 1710.*

The Archangel Raphael's name means "God has healed," and he appears most thoroughly in the Book of Tobit, which is in the Roman Catholic Bible. One [...] to seek cure for [...] meets the archangel [...] fish that [...] also assist him in [...] has five husbands [...] This was not her fault [...] to be vanquished [...] reading Rafael [...] troubled the waters of [...] the New [...] he often is feasted [...] September 29 San Rafael [...] modified [...] each [...] archangel [...] holding a fish [...] patron of druggists, health inspectors, lovers, travelers, and young people leaving home, he is also invoked again[...]

SAN RAFAEL ARCÁNGEL

THE ARCHANGEL RAPHAEL

✢ THE ARCHANGEL RAPHAEL'S NAME means "God has healed," and he appears most thoroughly in the Book of Tobit, which is in the Catholic Bible. On his way to seek a cure for his father's blindness, young Tobias meets the archangel in disguise. Rafael helps him catch the huge fish that cures the father's blindness, and also assists him in winning the beautiful Sara, whose previous five husbands did not survive their wedding nights. This was not her fault but that of a demon who needed to be vanquished. It's a lovely story, and one that bears reading. Rafael also is believed to be the angel who troubled the waters of the healing pool of Bethesda (John 5:1-4) in the New Testament.

His day is October 24, but he often is feasted, along with Saint Michael, on September 29.

San Rafael is depicted as a winged young man often clad in modified Roman armor and leggings—the usual garb for archangels in this tradition. He is usually shown holding a fish or helping Tobias land the fish. He is patron of druggists, health inspectors, lovers, travelers, and young people leaving home; he is also invoked against blindness.

OPPOSITE: *This painting of San Rafael, painted by Zoraida Ortega, appears on the main altar of Eulogio and Zoraida Ortega's private Guadalupe chapel in Velarde, New Mexico.*

THE
GUARDIAN
ANGEL

✛ ACCORDING TO POPULAR BELIEF, every person is watched over by an angel. As messengers of God, the guardian angels watch over their individual charges, represent them before God, help them in prayer, and keep them from stumbling or falling on life's pathway. After death, the souls of the just are presented to God by their guardian angels. As Psalm 91:11-12 tells us, "For to his angels he has given command about you, that they guard you in all your ways. Upon their hands shall they bear you up, lest you dash your foot against a stone." Guardian angels have their day on October 2.

Images of el Ángel de la Guardia are particularly popular in the chapels and churches that dot the Tohono O'odham Nation in southern Arizona. Most are purchased just across the border in the regional pilgrimage center of Magdalena, Sonora. They usually show a little boy and girl, often dressed in Alpine costume, either crossing a chasm on a rickety wooden bridge or leaning over the abyss to pick a flower. The angel towers behind and over them to ensure that no harm befall them. A touching image, and, in the middle of the Sonoran Desert, a rather startling one.

OPPOSITE: *The illustration shows an image of el Ángel de la Guardia purchased in Magdalena, Sonora. It is set in a glass frame painted by Anastacio León of Imuris, Sonora. León is one of a handful of traditional craftspeople in the region who create decorative frames to sell to the O'odham for their chapels. The designs are painted on the back of the glass in both opaque and translucent colors. The glass is then backed with crumpled aluminum foil, which gives a wonderful glimmering effect to the piece. Here, the angel's wings and clothing have been embellished further with glitter.*

036 Angel de la Guarda

✦ THE IMMACULATE CONCEPTION represents neither an episode in the life of the Virgin, like Our Lady of Sorrows, nor a specific apparition, such as the Virgin of Guadalupe. Rather, she commemorates the concept that Mary was conceived totally free of the Original Sin that we inherited from our First Parents and which weighs us down. This aspect of Mary has been a part of Catholic belief since the early seventeenth century, and Catholic doctrine since 1854. Thus, by the time Catholicism became established in what are now the border states, the belief was a solid part of Catholic thought. December 8 is the day on which this aspect of Mary is celebrated.

THE IMMACULATE CONCEPTION

La Purísima Concepción is usually represented as a woman with her hands folded and sometimes holding a flower. She often is clothed in blue and white, crowned, and standing on an angel-supported crescent moon or on a serpent. This last is a reference to the Woman of the Book of Revelation, and to the fact that—being totally without stain of sin—Mary vanquished the Evil One who tempted Eve in the Garden.

The old mission church in Caborca, Sonora, is dedicated to la Purísima Concepción. In 1857, the church was besieged by troops under the command of the American filibuster Henry Alexander Crabbe. According to local tradition, Crabbe's men tried to blow in the door of the church with a barrel of gunpowder. Each time they would light the fuse and take cover, a lady dressed in blue would appear and extinguish the spark. Thus did the Virgin successfully protect her church and her people.

OPPOSITE: *This statue of La Purísima Concepción stands in the church of San Miguel de Horcasitas, Sonora. Her earrings are said to have been given to her by a Yaqui Indian.*

ABOVE: *This statue of La Purísima Concepción stands in the east transept of Mission San Xavier del Bac, just south of Tucson, Arizona. It originally was housed at the mission church at Tumacácori, some forty miles south, the ruins of which are now preserved as a unit of Tumacácori National Historical Park.*

✦ THE VIRGIN MARY IS SAID to have appeared to an English Carmelite, Saint Simon Stock, in 1251. She showed him a brown scapular and told him that whomever wore these two squares of cloth over their shoulders would assuredly go to heaven under her personal protection. Her day is July 16.

Our Lady of Mount Carmel is depicted as crowned, and holding the Christ Child in one hand and a brown scapular in the other. Sometimes she wears the brown dress of the Carmelites. The Holy Child also may be crowned, and often holds a scapular. Souls in Purgatory are often depicted around the Virgin's feet, imploring to be rescued. In New Mexico, believers appeal to Nuestra Señora del Carmen for help against all dangers, especially in the hour of death. She also has the power to intercede for souls in Purgatory.

Our Lady of Mount Carmel

OPPOSITE: *Nuestra Señora del Carmen in the church of San Miguel Horcasitas, Sonora.*

LEFT: *This statue of Nuestra Señora del Carmen stands near the door of the colonial mission church of San Lorenzo de Huepac, in the valley of the Río Sonora. She has been given a bouquet of fresh flowers, and she and her Child are dressed in new finery. In her right hand she holds a scapular, with her image clearly visible.*

Nuestra Señora de la Paz
"La Conquistadora"

✦ "La Conquistadora" is a uniquely New Mexican manifestation of the Virgin Mary as Our Lady of Peace. Her story begins in 1625, when Fray Alonzo de Benavides brought a small statue of the Assumption of the Virgin to Santa Fe, New Mexico. The statue was short and slender, representing Mary as she was borne to heaven by angels. In Santa Fe, the statue came under the care of the confraternity of the Immaculate Conception. The Virgin's name was changed accordingly, and changed again when the confraternity changed its dedication to the rosary. At this time, in the mid-seventeenth century, the custom of dressing the statue in sumptuous clothing began—a custom that continues to this day. It was also at this time that the statue acquired its title of "La Conquistadora," because the Virgin had come to New Mexico with the original Spanish conquistadors, or conquerors.

In 1680, the sorely tried Pueblo peoples revolted and drove the Spaniards down the Rio Grande to the site of present-day El Paso, Texas. The statue of La Conquistadora also made the journey, only to return in 1691, when Spaniards under Diego de Vargas retook the region. Thus, her title was given new meaning. She eventually was housed in the parish church, on the site of what was to become the Saint Francis Cathedral.

Our Lady of Peace

There she remains, in a chapel all her own, dressed in rich costumes that are changed with each passing season. She has a new official title, however—Our Lady of Peace—which was given her recently in an effort to downplay her past association with military conquest and to establish her as a conqueror of the hearts of her people—who include everyone. So there she is, changing yet changeless, reflecting the history of New Mexico. Assumption, Immaculate Conception, Rosary, Conqueror, Lady of Peace—she has been all these things. Go to Santa Fe, New Mexico, during its annual Fiesta and see her being carried in procession through the streets of the city, or visit her in her chapel.

OPPOSITE: *La Conquistadora, dressed in early spring attire, in her chapel in Santa Fe, New Mexico.*

✝ ACCORDING TO DOMINICAN TRADITION, the Virgin Mary appeared to Saint Dominic (1170-1221) in a vision and taught him how to pray the rosary as it is prayed today. In 1571, when Christian forces definitively defeated the Turkish fleet at the battle of Lepanto, the Christian victory was attributed to the fact that large groups of the faithful in Rome prayed the rosary while the battle raged. For that reason, Our Lady of the Rosary is celebrated on October 7, the anniversary of that important battle.

Nuestra Señora del Rosario is depicted as holding the Holy Child in one hand and a rosary in the other. She is usually crowned, and stands on a crescent moon. Sometimes she is shown giving the rosary to Saint Dominic. She is patron of the Philippine Navy, and as such bears the title of "La Naval." In northern New Mexico she is petitioned for acceptance of death in the family, for peace, for protection from accidents, and for help in time of danger. A public praying of the rosary is a regular feature of wakes, which helps explain the connection with acceptance of death.

Our Lady of the Rosary

OPPOSITE: *This painting of Nuestra Señora del Rosario is in the east transept of Mission San Xavier del Bac, near Tucson, Arizona. An anonymous artist painted it in the mid-1790s.*

✦ **Our Lady of Sorrows** represents the Virgin Mary as she stands at the foot of the cross, mourning her Son who has just been executed by the Roman authorities. She usually has her face turned upward and to her left, and she clasps her hands in grief in front of her bosom. She may wear a silver crown, and she may have a dagger symbolizing her grief protruding from her heart. Alternatively, there may be seven daggers, symbolizing the Seven Sorrows of Mary. She often wears black to symbolize her mourning, although in some cases—such as at Mission San Xavier del Bac near Tucson, Arizona, she wears rich, light-colored garments. Her feasts are Friday of Passion Week and September 15.

She is believed to be especially concerned with children, with women in childbirth, and with sinners. Women turn to her in times of grief. Because she has gone through sorrow unimaginable, she can empathize with the grief of others.

Almost every Spanish colonial mission church in the region is equipped with a life-sized statue of the Sorrowing Mother. One reason for this may be that these statues often played a role in the Good Friday processions that missionaries, especially the Jesuits, used to dramatize the Passion story to their Indian converts.

Our Lady of Sorrows

OPPOSITE: *This statue of Nuestra Señora de Dolores, crowned and with her heart pierced by a silver dagger, stands in the mission church of La Asunción de Opodepe, in Sonora's San Miguel Valley.*

RIGHT: *Nuestra Señora de Dolores at Mission San Xavier del Bac near Tucson, Arizona.*

Nuestra Señora de Guadalupe

THE Virgin OF Guadalupe

✛ In December 1531, only a few years after the conquest of Mexico and the destruction of the Aztec universe, an Indian convert named Juan Diego was walking past a hill called Tepeyac, which in the old days had been dedicated to the Aztec goddess Tonantzin, "Our Mother." He heard his name called, and, looking over to the hillside, he saw a beautiful woman who told him that she was the Virgin Mary, the mother of God. She told Juan to go to Bishop Zumárraga in Mexico City and tell him to build a church for her on the spot where she had appeared. The bishop, unimpressed, twice denied Juan's request and insisted on seeing a sign of some sort. During a third apparition, the Virgin instructed Juan Diego to gather the roses he found growing on the hillside and take them to the bishop. As Juan dumped the flowers at the bishop's feet, he discovered that the image of the Virgin had miraculously imprinted itself on the cloak, or tilma, which he had used to carry the roses.

This tilma, which still hangs in the Basilica of Nuestra Señora de Guadalupe, bears the image of a dark-skinned young woman, eyes downcast and hands folded. She is shown surrounded by rays of light, clad in a robe bearing stars, and standing on the crescent moon.

Nuestra Señora de Guadalupe appears in churches, of course, and on home altars, but also is printed on T-shirts and painted on trees, road cuts, murals, and low-rider cars. She can be found at political rallies and union marches. She truly has transcended religion to become a living symbol of Mexican identity. Her day, December 12, is celebrated with special Masses, processions, and dramatic presentations.

OPPOSITE: *Shrine near Casas Grandes, Chihuahua. Each statue, candle, rosary, photograph, or other gift represents a request for a miracle.*

ABOVE: *Nuestra Señora de Guadalupe on the west wall of Menlo Park Video store in Tucson, Arizona, is the work of a well-known local muralist, David Tineo.*

✛ BORN IN LISBON, PORTUGAL, IN 1195, Saint Anthony (originally named Ferdinand) took up the religious life at an early age, becoming first an Augustinian and then, in 1221, a Franciscan. He was famous for his preaching, by means of which he reformed the city of Padua, and earned the nickname "the Wonder Worker" for the many miracles he is believed to have wrought. He also worked to abolish debtors' prisons and helped the poor. Saint Anthony died in 1231, was canonized the following year, and was named a Doctor of the Church in 1946. His feast day is June 13.

SAINT ANTHONY OF PADUA

Patron of the poor and oppressed, of harvests, and of the country of Portugal, Saint Anthony also is invoked to help find lost articles. Legend has it that a disciple who took Saint Anthony's psalter without asking permission was visited by terrifying apparitions until he returned the book, hence the popular prayer: "Saint Anthony, Saint Anthony, look around/Something's lost and can't be found." He is also invoked by spinsters seeking husbands and by childless women wishing to become pregnant. He is depicted wearing a Franciscan habit and often is shown cradling the Christ Child, who is said to have appeared to him.

Franciscan missionaries most probably brought the devotion to San Antonio to the region in the seventeenth century, and his image appears at many historic churches that were once Franciscan missions.

San Antonio is the beloved patron of the church and village of Oquitoa, Sonora. According to local legend, in the 1830s, Indians attacking Oquitoa retreated when they saw what they believed to be a column of cavalry coming to the rescue. Leading the phantom charge was a bald-headed officer with a gray cloak: San Antonio, tonsured and wearing his gray Franciscan habit.

OPPOSITE: *This image of San Antonio is from Mission San Xavier del Bac, just south of Tucson, Arizona, and has been standing in its niche in the east transept since the church was dedicated in 1797. The rosary in the saint's hand is probably an offering.*

ABOVE: *San Antonio by New Mexico santera Arlene Sena.*

Saint Augustine was one of the most influential writers and thinkers ... Afric... in 3... war... bec... se... rely... stic... wa... baptiz... su... pre... er an... inclu... Con...essions... ne is ...pon... si... for the... ...inati... he... a ve... Docto... Chu... h, his... folk... us... M...diterra... a hol... with... sa... The... buck... on the... and... ad d...e... A...g... p...ce a... on the... vis... them. Since I can't s...im, I'm emptying the sea so I can wal... across. "Little boy, that's ridiculous," said San Agustín...

✝ SAINT AUGUSTINE was one of the most influential writers and thinkers in the history of Christianity. Born in North Africa in 354 of a pagan father and a devout Christian mother, who was to become Saint Monica, he led a dissolute youth. After several religious experiments, he embraced Christianity and was baptized in 387. He enjoyed phenomenal success as a preacher and wrote a series of important books, including his *Confessions* and *The City of God*. Saint Augustine is responsible for the doctrines of Original Sin and predestination, and he held a very low view of women in general. He is the patron of theologians, brewers, and printers. A Doctor of the Church, his feast day is August 28.

A Spanish folktale tells us that San Agustín, walking along the shore of the Mediterranean one day, saw a little boy digging a hole in the sand. The boy then proceeded to fill bucket after bucket from the sea and pour the contents into the hole he had dug. San Agustín asked the boy what he was doing.

"My parents are on the island of Cyprus," replied the lad, "and I want to visit them. Since I can't swim, I'm emptying the sea so I can walk across."

"Little boy, that's ridiculous!" said San Agustín. The Boy looked him right in the eye.

"Not as ridiculous as you were, San Agustín, when you tried to explain the Trinity!" He replied.

OPPOSITE: *On the façade of the San Agustín Cathedral in Tucson, Arizona, the city's patron is depicted dressed as a bishop, holding a crozier. Other traditional symbols include a dove and a shell. The medallions to left and right of his feet contain the lion of Saint Mark and the ox of Saint Luke. A Sonoran desert scene appears in relief below, with San Xavier Mission on the far right.*

ABOVE: *This statue, created by William Hawes Smith for the Arizona Historical Society's annual Fiesta de San Agustín, awaits a procession in his honor.*

✛ ACCORDING TO LEGEND, Saint Barbara lived in the third or fourth century and was the daughter of a wealthy pagan. When she converted to Christianity, her father locked her in a tower. There she built three windows, to honor the Trinity. Enraged by her continuing devotion, he had her tortured and killed and was himself destroyed by fire from heaven, in the form of a lightning flash. Historically, all we know for certain about Barbara is her name. For this reason, the church removed her from the active Calendar of Saints in 1969. Nevertheless, many still celebrate her feast day on December 4.

Saint Barbara is depicted wearing a crown and holding a monstrance and the palm of martyrdom. Her dress often has three flounces, probably symbolizing the Trinity. A tower, often with three windows, and a storm cloud and lightning bolt may be in the background. She protects against lightning and also is the patroness of artillerymen and those, such as miners, who work with explosives. Having transformed her tower prison into a shrine to the Trinity, she also has an affinity for architects, builders, and stone masons.

SAINT BARBARA

OPPOSITE: *This statue of Santa Bárbara resides in the home of New Mexico santero Charlie Carrillo. Alcario Otero of Tomé, New Mexico, friend and former student of Carillo, was the artist.*

✝ SAINT CAJETAN WAS BORN in Vicenza, Italy, in 1480 and studied at the University of Padua, where he received doctorates in civil and canon law. He was ordained a priest in 1516 and thereafter ministered to the poor, the sick, and especially the incurable. In 1524, he helped found the Theatine Institute, which was devoted to preaching, aiding the sick, and reforming the Church. He later helped found an institution to help the poor by pawning goods at low interest. He died in 1547, and his feast day is August 7.

It would seem natural that San Cayetano would be the patron saint of pawnbrokers, but in the American Southwest he is patron of gamblers as well. This may be because gamblers, often in need of ready cash, were especially grateful for his low-interest pawn-shops. People used to bet him a rosary or a blessed candle that he would not perform some miracle. In southern Arizona, he is invoked to help find lost objects. Once again, the custom is to bet him some small thing—a prayer, a candle, or even the specific sum of eleven

SAINT CAJETAN

cents—that he can't find the needed object. He is said not to be able to resist this challenge. San Cayetano is shown wearing a black cassock, often with a jeweled collar or necklace. In New Mexico, he can be depicted wearing a flat, black hat. He sometimes carries a palm and kneels next to a table while holding a cross.

Although San Cayetano is quite popular in the American Southwest, representations of him are fairly rare. One of the few can be found in the Santuario at Chimayó, north of Santa Fe; New Mexico, and another is in the nearby church of Santa Cruz de la Cañada. A third is in the church at San Acacio, Colorado, at the northern edge of Spanish settlement in the nineteenth century.

OPPOSITE: *Repeated Apache raids forced missionaries and parishioners to abandon the mission at Tumacácori in December, 1848, and this statue—slightly charred from a fire—was brought up to Mission San Xavier del Bac near Tucson, Arizona. There it knelt in the west transept until the 1970s, when was returned to Tumacácori National Historical Park, where it now stands in the museum.*

✝ BORN IN 1194 OF A NOBLE FAMILY in Assisi, Italy, Saint Clare was so impressed when she heard Saint Francis of Assisi preach that she ran away from home at the age of twelve to become one of his followers. When her sister Agnes joined her, their furious parents sent armed men to bring them back. Clare's prayers caused Agnes to become so heavy that she could not be moved. Clare and her followers formed the female branch of the Franciscan movement—the Poor Clares, taking strict vows of poverty. She is credited with many miracles and, after Saint Francis himself, is the person most responsible for the growth and spread of the Franciscans. She died in 1253 after years of illness and suffering, and was canonized two years later. Her feast day is August 11.

SAINT CLARE

Santa Clara usually is shown wearing a Franciscan habit and holding a monstrance. Because she embroidered altar clothes and other church materials while she was ill, she is revered as patron of embroiderers. She also had a vision of the Christmas Crib as she lay on her sickbed one Christmas Eve, which led Pope Pius XII to name her patroness of television. Her popular devotion is particularly strong in northern New Mexico, where the Franciscans were in charge from the sixteenth to the nineteenth centuries.

OPPOSITE: *This candle was purchased at a Tucson, Arizona, store that specializes in medicinal herbs and other materials associated with healing. Similar candles are placed as offerings at countless shrines and altars throughout the region.*

San Francisco de Asís

✝ Born in 1181 to a wealthy merchant of Assisi, Francis spent his youth in high living and soldiering until a vision of Christ changed his entire life. Thereafter, he devoted himself to a life of poverty and the care of the sick and poor. After his father disinherited him, he attracted followers and began the order of Friars Minor, popularly known as the Franciscans. He advocated a life of total poverty and service to God, and is notable for seeing all life forms—including fire and, eventually, Sister Death—as his siblings under God. In an ecstatic vision, he received the stigmata, or wounds identical to those of Christ. He had a strong devotion to the Christ Child and helped popularize the Christmas Crib, or nativity scene, complete with animals. In legend, he preached to the birds and persuaded a wolf not to eat people. Few saints have influenced the course of Christianity to the extent that Francis did. He died in 1226, and his feast is celebrated on October 4.

San Francisco usually is shown in two ways. The older, Hispanic representations have him kneeling with outstretched arms, receiving the stigmata, or standing with a skull in his hand. In either case, he is wearing a gray or blue habit, belted with a knotted cord. More recent representations show him in a brown habit, which is the dress of modern Franciscans, with small birds and animals perched on his shoulders.

Pope John Paul II proclaimed San Francisco de Asís patron of the ecology movement in 1979, and he is invoked to restore peace among family members. He also is the patron of Santa Fe, New Mexico, the full name of which is La Ciudad Real de la Santa Fe de San Francisco de Asís—the Royal City of the Holy Faith of Saint Francis of Assisi.

SAINT FRANCIS OF ASSISI

OPPOSITE: *The painting of San Francisco is part of the altar at Manny Gurulé's private chapel near Santa Fe, New Mexico, and was done by New Mexico santero Frankie Lucero. By including both a skull and a bird in flight, the artist has referred to both the older and the more recent conceptions of the saint.*

LEFT: *The statue of Saint Francis holding the birds stands outside Saint Francis in the Foothills, a Methodist Church in Tucson, Arizona.*

✦ BORN NEAR PAMPLONA in the Basque country of Spain in 1506, Saint Francis Xavier studied in Paris and while there was greatly influenced Saint Ignatius Loyola. A first-generation Jesuit, Xavier was sent as a missionary to the East Indies. He spread the Gospel in Goa, the southern tip of India, the Spice Islands, the Philippines, and Japan. He died in 1552 on an island off the coast of China, a land he had hoped to reach but never did. His body was packed in lime and returned by sea to Goa, where it is said to have arrived in a perfect state of preservation. The faithful took this as a sign of Xavier's strong spiritual qualities. His body still lies in state in the church of Bom Jesus in Goa, where thousands of pilgrims each year celebrate his feast day on December 3.

San Francisco Xavier was the personal patron of Father Eusebio Francisco Kino, the Jesuit missionary who brought Christianity and European culture to much of present-day Arizona and Sonora.

SAINT FRANCIS XAVIER

But in the Sonoran Desert the story doesn't end there. A famous statue in the town of Magdalena de Kino, Sonora, the original of which may have been brought there by Father Kino himself, represents the saint lying on his deathbed. It also is interpreted as representing San Francisco Xavier's incorrupt body. This statue (BELOW) is believed by locals to represent a completely different San Francisco than the standing image of San Xavier. This composite saint, who seems to embody aspects of both Assisi and Xavier with a little bit of Padre Kino thrown in, is feasted on October 4—day of San Francisco Asís. Thousands of pilgrims wend their way to Magdalena, Sonora, each year for the fiesta dedicated to this folk creation, who is the informal patron of the entire Arizona–Sonora border region.

OPPOSITE: *San Francisco Xavier wears a biretta and holds a crucifix in both hands at Mission San Xavier del Bac near Tucson, Arizona.*

SAN YSIDRO LABRADOR

✛ BORN IN MADRID, SPAIN, Saint Isidore became the hired hand of a wealthy estate owner. He is said to have lived a life of great piety, performed miracles, and shared what little he had with the poor. The central legend told of him is that his employer objected to the amount of time during the day that he spent praying, rather than doing farm work. One day, when the boss came to check up on him, he found the saint on his knees praying, while an angel drove a team of snow-white oxen and guided the plow. In winter he would empty sacks of grain to feed the starving birds, and the sacks miraculously would be refilled with grain that would yield twice as much flour.

San Ysidro usually appears in farmer's work clothes, sometimes praying and sometimes holding a staff. Beside him, an angel plows with a team of oxen. In the ranching community of Meresechi, Sonora, the angel has two white-faced Herefords hitched to the plow. San Ysidro is the patron of farmers, ranchers, and crops, and is petitioned for rain. In times of extreme drought, his image may be taken from the church and carried around the fields to see the situation for himself; in truly severe cases, he may be buried and left until it rains again. His feast day, May 15, is important to residents throughout the ranching and farming country of the borderlands, and may be celebrated with processions and horse races. In some Sonoran communities, a special vegetable stew, which includes every kind of produce that is available at that season, is cooked in a huge pot and served on this day.

SAINT ISIDORE THE HUSBANDMAN

San Ysidro has a special connection with New Mexico. The wealthy estate owner for whom he worked, Juan de Vargas, is believed to have been a direct ancestor of Diego de Vargas, commander of the re-conquest of New Mexico following the Pueblo Revolt of 1680.

OPPOSITE: *This statue of San Ysidro Labrador stands near the doorway of the church of Nuestra Señora de la Candelaria in Villa de Seris, an old district of the Sonoran capital city of Hermosillo. It is almost life-sized, and of twentieth century origin.*

LEFT: *Statue by santero Manny Gurulé.*

✚ THE APOSTLE JAMES IS SAID by legend to have traveled to Spain, where he labored to convert the pagan peoples in the northwest corner of that peninsula. After his martyrdom in Jerusalem, his body was transported miraculously back to Spain, where it was discovered eight hundred years later at a site called Compostela, short for Campo de Estrellas or Field of Stars. Compostela is, after Jerusalem and Rome, the third great destination for Christian pilgrims, and attracts more than a hundred thousand visitors annually to celebrate his feast day, July 25.

The Galilean fisherman was seen as a valiant warrior who helped the Christian Spaniards in their long battle against the Moors, and for this reason he is referred to alternatively as Santiago Matamoros, or Saint James the Moor-killer. His name also was invoked during the militant expansion of Spanish Christianity throughout the Americas. Today he remains patron of the Spanish Army, horsemen, cock-fights, and Spain itself.

Santiago's symbol, the cockleshell, appears on many of the missions in the region. He himself often is depicted as a horseman, armed with lance or sword, cutting down his heathen enemies. Representations of him in militant guise, rather than as an apostle or a pilgrim, are more common in New Mexico. On the border, "Santiago" is a poetic term for the word given to start a horse race.

SAINT JAMES THE GREATER

OPPOSITE: *The famous statue of Santiago in the Santuario de Chimayó. It was made by an anonymous santero between 1810 and 1820 and repaired in 1955 by Alan Vedder of the Museum of New Mexico. It was once customary to leave miniature boots, bridles, quirts, and sombreros as offerings to this militant defender of Christian communities.*

LEFT: *New Mexican santero Nick Herrera's interpretation of Santiago on the altar of the private chapel of Manny Gurulé near Sante Fe, New Mexico.*

✦ SAINT JOHN THE BAPTIST was born to Zacharias, a priest in the Temple in Jerusalem, and his wife Elizabeth, who was a kinswoman of the Virgin Mary. He became a hermit in the desert, living on locusts and wild honey and preaching the coming of the Messiah and the need for repentance and baptism. When Christ came to him to be baptized, John recognized Him as the One for whose coming he had been preparing the people. King Herod later arrested John and had him beheaded at the request of his stepdaughter, Salome.

SAINT JOHN THE BAPTIST

San Juan Bautista is shown as a bearded man, dressed in a camel skin and often holding a staff. In many instances, a lamb accompanies him. He is the patron of road workers, leather workers, and wool workers, as well as of health spas. In the Sonoran Desert, June 24—el día de San Juan—is considered to be the first day on which the summer rains can begin. Some believe that if it rains on this day, the rainy season will be rich and wonderful; but if it rains just before the day, some sort of disaster may be in the offing.

On el día de San Juan, musicians traditionally would serenade everyone named Juan, Juana, John, or Jane at dawn, and people would picnic by whatever running water was available. Some still believe that because running water was used to baptize Jesus, it has special, curative powers on this special day. Though San Juan is seldom represented in churches, he remains important in the hearts and minds of people in this region, partly because of his association with water, without which there could be no life.

OPPOSITE: *San Juan Bautista stands in his portable case at the fiesta on el día de San Juan in Tucson, Arizona.*

✝ A CARPENTER BY TRADE, SAINT JOSEPH was the husband of Mary, the mother of Jesus. He was present at the birth of Christ and the Adoration of the Magi and helped nurture the Holy Child. The last reference to him in the scriptures occurs when he and Mary took young Jesus to the Temple in Jerusalem and lost track of Him, only to find Him disputing with the learned men. Saint Joseph's feast day is March 19.

Tradition often envisions San José as an old man, but in the American Southwest he is usually depicted as being younger. He is bearded and usually cradles the Christ Child in one arm while holding a flowering staff in his other hand. Legend has it that when the various suitors of the Virgin Mary left their walking sticks in the synagogue, the staff of San Jose bloomed as a sign that he was the one chosen for the great task of helping raise the Son of God. In more contemporary representations, he sometimes holds a carpenter's square.

San José is patron of a happy death because, according to legend, Christ was with him at the time of his death. He also speaks for fathers, families, travelers, carpenters, and, by extension, all workers. In the twentieth century, his aid was enlisted to help workers resist the temptations of Communist doctrine.

In the Southwest, homeowners and real estate agents seeking to attract prospective buyers have taken to burying a small statue of San José in the yard, often upside down.

SAINT JOSEPH

OPPOSITE: *This statue of Saint Joseph the Carpenter stands in the Peace Shrine in Yarnell, Arizona. It was created in the 1950s by the late Felix Lucero, who is better known for making the statues illustrating the life of Christ that stand in the Garden of Gethsemane on the west bank of the Santa Cruz River in Tucson, Arizona. After Lucero was spared from death on the Western Front in World War I, he spent many of his remaining years creating religious art as an act of gratitude.*

ABOVE: *San José and El Santo Niño by Charlie Carrillo in the church of Our Lady Queen of Peace in Santa Fe, New Mexico.*

✛ A BROTHER OF SAINT JAMES, and therefore possibly of Jesus as well, Saint Jude also was one of the Twelve Apostles. Legend has him preaching in Mesopotamia and being martyred in Persia. Little else seems to be known concerning this rather shadowy saint, who for a long time was ignored in the prayers of the faithful—possibly because he bore the same name as Judas Iscariot, betrayer of Jesus. His feast day is October 28.

SAINT JUDE

San Judas is shown dressed in a long green robe, with a holy medal (often a huge one) on his chest. A flame of enlightenment springs from his forehead. He sometimes is shown with an anchor and an oar, because he was a fisherman. The anchor also is a symbol of hope. He is famous nowadays as the patron of desperate situations and impossible causes, and as such has become very popular along the border, with representations of him outnumbering those of San Martín de Porres, another saint invoked by those who feel themselves to be in hopeless straits. Although he is seen rarely in northern New Mexico, he appears on storefronts in Tucson, Arizona, and in front yard shrines. His is the most common image, after that of Nuestra Señora de Guadalupe, in roadside chapels in Sonora and Chihuahua, Mexico.

OPPOSITE: *This painting of San Judas occupies a vertical concrete slab beside the northbound lane of International Highway 15, just south of Cibuta, Sonora. Near it stand two chapels, one dedicated to the Virgin of Guadalupe, and the other dedicated to both the Virgin and San Judas. The votive candles at the base of the painting indicate that this site is used as a place of petitions by passers-by on the road to the international border.*

LEFT: *Tile mosaic on the façade of the Armando González family's San Judas capilla in Tucson, Arizona.*

BLESSED KATERI TEKAKWITHA

✛ THIS YOUNG SEVENTEENTH-CENTURY Mohawk woman is on her way to becoming the first Native American saint in the Catholic Church. She was declared "Blessed" in 1980 by Pope John Paul II, and her many followers have high hopes that she will soon take the final step to full saint-hood. Already, her image appears on many altars and in churches with a preponderance of Native American worshippers.

Kateri was born in New York state in 1656 and orphaned at an early age by an epidemic of smallpox, which also left her terribly disfigured. She was converted to Catholicism by a French Jesuit missionary in 1676 and, fearing for her life, walked the two hundred miles to a Christian Indian village near Montreal. In 1679, she took a vow of chastity and devotion to Christ. She died the next year, greatly respected for her holiness and concern for others. Many miracles are attributed to this "Lily of the Mohawks," as she is known.

Blessed Kateri is the special patroness of all Catholic Native Americans and is serving to unite native peoples from all parts of North America. Although she was native to upstate New York, in recent years her devotion has spread everywhere that Indian peoples live. She is shown as a young woman, clad in buckskin and holding a cross.

OPPOSITE: *This image hangs between the door and the altar of Saint Nicholas Indian Center in South Tucson, Arizona, one of the chapels in a widespread Blessed Kateri Tekakwitha parish that serves Tohono O'odham, Yaquis, and people of other tribes. It was carved by Eleanor H. Bruegel of Broomall, Pennsylvania. The painted cross and other motifs in the background are the work of Leonard Chana, a Tohono O'odham artist.*

SPQR

DONADO POR:
SUS DEVOTOS

✛ SAINT LAWRENCE WAS A DEACON of the church who suffered martyrdom in Rome in 258, during the reign of the emperor Valerian. Hearing a prediction that he would be killed in three days, he sold many of the church's possessions and distributed the money to the poor and the sick. When Roman authorities demanded that he turn over to them all the church's property, he assembled all of these needy folks and announced that *they* were the treasures of the church. He was literally cooked on a gridiron, a fate that he suffered with incredible calm. It is said that at one point he asked the executioner to turn him over, as he was well done on one side. His death signaled a general conversion to Christianity in Rome. His day is August 10.

SAINT LAWRENCE

San Lorenzo is shown dressed in red, with a martyr's palm and a grill either in his hands or beside him. He is the patron of Sri Lanka (formerly Ceylon), librarians, cooks, and the poor. He also is invoked to help crops survive the heat of August and to fight and prevent fires. He is of considerable importance on both sides of the border in the greater El Paso–Ciudad Juárez area, with churches in suburban Clint, Texas, and San Lorenzo, Chihuahua, dedicated to him. His fiesta is a major event at both of these sites.

OPPOSITE: *This stained glass window is in the church of San Lorenzo in Clint, Texas. It depicts the moment of San Lorenzo's martyrdom. Roman soldiers light the flames, stir the coals, and watch impassively, while the dove of the Holy Spirit consoles the dying but steadfast saint. One soldier holds a legionary standard bearing an eagle and the letters S.P.Q.R. The initials stand for "Senatus Populusque Romanus"—"the senate and the people of Rome." The eagle was the semi-sacred symbol of each Roman legion.*

ABOVE: *Statue in the side chapel of the church of San Lorenzo in Clint, Texas.*

Martin of Porres was born in Lima, Peru
1579. His father was a Spanish knight and his mother
Panamanian freed...   African descent, who
Martin favored his ...   and complexion
was apprenticed ...   at age fifteen
entered a Domin...   came a professed
brother. He wo...   menial tasks
showed deep co...   of the hu...
...cies, but als...   such verm...
ats and mice.   and cats at his
...'s house, c...   slaves rece...
...rived from ...   an orphanage
...oundling hos...   lieved to have
...fts of levita...   latter ability
...two places a...   or a hard-work
...ervice-oriented ...   Martin. An inten
...umble man, he re...   as Brother Broo
...e died in 1639, and ...   lebrated on Novemb
...gnition was long in coming for this decent, de...

✝ SAINT MARTIN OF PORRES was born in Lima, Peru, in 1579. His father was a Spanish knight and his mother was a Panamanian freedwoman of African descent, whom Saint Martin favored in features and complexion. He was apprenticed to a barber-surgeon, but at age fifteen he entered a Dominican friary, where he became a professed lay brother. He worked at a succession of menial tasks and showed deep concern not only for the poor of the human species, but also for other animals and even vermin such as rats and mice. He kept a hospice for dogs and cats at his sister's house, cared for the sick and for slaves recently arrived from Africa, and helped establish an orphanage and foundling hospital in Lima.

SAINT MARTIN OF PORRES

He was believed to have the gifts of levitation and of bilocation. This latter ability to be in two places at once was a great boon for a hard-working, service-oriented person like Saint Martin. An intensely humble man, he referred to himself as "Brother Broom." He died in 1639, and he is celebrated on November 3.

Recognition was long in coming for this decent, dedicated man. San Martín de Porres was not beatified until 1837, and was not recognized officially as a saint until 1962. He is patron of social justice and of people of mixed race, as well as of hairdressers and of public education and television in Peru. In the Mexican world, those on the bottom of the socio-economic order view him as a true friend and helper. He is shown as a Negro, wearing a black-and-white Dominican habit.

San Martín was extremely popular in the years following his canonization, but recently he seems to have been eclipsed in popularity by Saint Jude. His image can be found in the eighteenth-century mission churches of Sonora—but figures of him are rare in northern New Mexico, where he has not achieved great popularity.

OPPOSITE: *This statue of San Martín de Porres stands in a chapel built in his honor in Casa Blanca, Sonora, a tiny settlement south of Santa Ana on International Highway 15.*

ABOVE: *Statue in the side chapel of the church of San Lorenzo in Clint, Texas.*

✛ SAINT MARTIN OF TOURS was a conscripted Roman soldier who was born about 316. Around 337, while stationed near Amiens in Gaul, he took pity on a ragged roadside beggar, cut his cloak in half with his sword, and gave half the cloak to the stranger. Later that night, Christ appeared to him in his sleep wearing the half of the cloak he had given to the beggar. Saint Martin thereupon became a Christian and left the army. He then spent many years as a hermit until he was assigned, rather against his will, to be Bishop of Tours. There he founded an important monastery and converted many to Christianity while destroying pagan places of worship in the process. He was said to have experienced visions and to have the gift of prophecy. Saint Martin was an important figure in the history of early Western monasticism, and his shrine was a major pilgrimage center during the Middle Ages. He died in 397, and his feast is celebrated on November 11.

San Martín Caballero is shown wearing Roman armor and sitting on his horse, in the act of cutting his cloak in half for the old man with a white beard who crouches beside him. He is the patron of soldiers, beggars, horsemen, innkeepers, winegrowers, drunkards, and geese, among other things.

In the Mexican world, San Martín also is the patron of business people, and many stores and restaurants in the border states have an altar to him somewhere on the premises. At such altars, many people will place a bit of grass or hay and a small container of water—for the horse. Everyone knows that, in this arid cattle country of the "far north," horses must be fed and watered. As long as there's fodder and water for San Martín's horse, the kitchen will never lack for food and drink. Saints, it would seem, can fend for themselves.

SAINT MARTIN OF TOURS

OPPOSITE: *In the Little Mexico restaurant in Tucson, Arizona, San Martín Caballero occupies a particularly lovely tin nicho, imported from Mexico. The water cup is visible on the right, and the grass is in the center. Dollar bills at the left are the first ones the proprietors took in when the business opened and are a gift to San Martín.*

✝ BORN IN SPAIN IN 1540, Saint Paschal Baylon was a shepherd who taught himself to read and write. The Franciscans initially refused to accept him into their order, but Saint Paschal was admitted as a lay brother on his second try in 1564. He spent most of the next twenty-eight years as a porter in different friaries in Spain and was known for his charity, humility, and devotion to the poor and the sick. He had a particular devotion to the Eucharist and is said to have died at the very moment the Host was being consecrated in the nearby church. His feast is May 17.

Officially, he is the patron of the Eucharist and of Eucharistic congresses, of Italian women, and of shepherds. Quite unofficially, in Mexico, he also is well known as the patron of kitchens because legend has it that an angel attended to his kitchen duties while he prayed before the Eucharist. He usually is shown wearing a Franciscan habit. Sometimes he carries a

SAINT PASCHAL BAYLON

shepherd's crook, and often he is depicted as adoring a Host in a monstrance. In Mexican representations, there usually is a tiled stove behind him, with a pot over the flames.

How San Pascual became popular in New Mexico is not certain. American artists in the Santa Fe, New Mexico, area may have seen representations of him in Mexico and, wanting a saint for their kitchens, asked Hispanic artists to reproduce his image. What is certain is that his arrival in New Mexico post-dates World War II, and he appears in more Anglo kitchens than Hispanic ones. In fact, his increased importance in Anglo circles may well coincide with the rise in popularity of gourmet cooking in the American Southwest.

OPPOSITE: *This statue of San Pascual with his cooking pots resides in the Santa Fe, New Mexico, home of santero Charlie Carrillo. It was carved of cedar by Taos santero Ricardo P. Salazar.*

✝ SAINT PETER WAS ONE OF THE ORIGINAL twelve apostles. Rash and impetuous, he is, after Jesus, the most fully developed character in the gospels. He had enough faith to walk on water, yet he doubted enough that he began to sink. He grabbed a sword and cut off the ear of a man who came to arrest Christ in the Garden of Gethsemane, but then he denied Jesus three times before the cock crowed. It was to this very human person that Christ entrusted His church, making him in effect the first pope. Legend has him arriving in Rome with his wife and daughter and being crucified upside down, by his request, during the reign of Emperor Nero. Ever after, the Bishop of Rome has been recognized as leader of the Roman Catholic Church. Saint Peter's feast day is June 29.

San Pedro usually is shown as an old man with a white beard. He holds keys in his right hand, because Christ entrusted him with the keys to the kingdom of heaven. He also may carry a book. A rooster often stands somewhere in the background. He is patron of clockmakers, boat builders, fishermen, and net makers. Believers appeal to him for long life, and he is invoked for foot trouble, fever, and for protection from wolves. In New Mexico, he also has been petitioned to free prisoners and to ensure a happy death and admission to heaven.

SAINT PETER

OPPOSITE: *This elaborate painting of San Pedro hangs on a road cut in the southbound lane of International Highway 15, just south of Cibuta, Sonora. The saint holds his keys and gazes towards heaven. A rooster crows on a wall behind him and to his right. Above him, from left to right, are San Judas, the reclining San Francisco as he is venerated in nearby Magdalena, Sonora, and El Santo Niño. This particular red-clad representation of the Christ Child with His arms raised is called El Divino Niño—"The Divine Child."*

San Ramón Nonato

✦ SAINT RAYMOND WAS BORN around 1204 in Catalonia, Spain. He was delivered by caesarian section after his mother's death, and for that reason bears the second name of Nonnatus, meaning "not born." He joined the Mercedarian Order, whose self-imposed task was to ransom Christian slaves who had been captured by Muslims. While acting as hostage for several slaves who had been released pending payment, Raymond converted several Muslims to Christianity and was sentenced to death. His sentence was commuted; he was forced to run the gauntlet instead and was further tortured by having his lips drilled through with a red-hot poker and padlocked together. Finally ransomed, Saint Raymond returned to Barcelona in 1239 and was appointed a cardinal. He died in 1240 en route to Rome to accept his appointment. He was canonized in 1657, and his feast is August 31.

San Ramón is the patron of midwives and those falsely accused of crimes, and is called upon in cases of difficult childbirth. In New Mexico, he was of special comfort to the colonists who lived in constant fear of being captured and tortured by Apaches, Comanches, and other Indian raiders.

There is a small chapel to San Ramón on the main route south through Nogales, Sonora. By the 1980s the chapel, once well out of town, was in the midst of a busy district of maquiladoras—assembly plants that take advantage of the tax-free border zone and Mexico's lower labor costs. Eventually, the chapel was torn down and the front wall of such a plant was erected over the place where it had stood. According to a local story, the front wall of the factory, which ran right through the chapel site, kept falling down as soon as it was erected. The last time it collapsed, one of the men in charge of the construction work was killed. The building was then redesigned to avoid the chapel site, and a new chapel was erected on the site of the old one.

SAINT RAYMOND NONNATUS

OPPOSITE: *This painting of San Ramón Nonato, by New Mexican santero José Ramón López, hangs near the door of Eulogio and Zoraida Ortega's private chapel in Velarde, New Mexico.*

Santa Rita

✝ BORN IN ITALY IN 1381, SAINT RITA was married at the age of twelve to an abusive husband. She lived with him faithfully for eighteen years and bore him two sons. After the husband was killed in a brawl and her sons died, she tried three times to become an Augustinian nun. Refused twice by that order on the grounds that she was not a virgin, she finally was accepted after being miraculously transported into the cloister. She became known for her austerity, acts of self-denial, and concern for others. Her prayers brought many people back to their religion. After hearing a sermon on the crown of thorns, she developed a wound in her forehead. She died in 1457 and was canonized in 1900. Her feast day is May 22.

She is patroness of desperate cases and is invoked in unhappy marriages, and against bleeding, infertility, loneliness, and tumors. In New Mexico, there was often the concern that too many petitions to her for patience would bring not only great patience but also a bad husband to provide the need for that virtue. She is depicted in a nun's habit, often carrying a cross and a skull, and with a thorn stuck in her forehead.

There is a shrine to Santa Rita near Amado, in southern Arizona's Santa Cruz River Valley. Across the valley to the east of the shrine loom the Santa Rita Mountains. Among the many visitors to the shrine are mothers of wayward children, who ask the saint's help for their loved ones. Although the shrine is not close to any house, it is always well-kept, and there are always candles burning at it.

SAINT RITA

OPPOSITE: *This painting is by New Mexican santero David Navor Lucero. It is part of the altar of the private chapel of Manny Gurulé's near Santa Fe, New Mexico* (LEFT).

✝ BORN AT ÁVILA IN 1515, SAINT TERESA entered the Carmelite Order at the age of twenty-one. She had visions and heard voices, which disturbed her until her confessor, Saint Peter of Alcantará, convinced her that these were of authentically Divine origin. Her mystical experiences were intense and often painful; she once experienced God's love like a lance driven deep into her heart. Deeply concerned about the relaxed attitude of many convents in her day, Teresa worked for reform within her order. She started what became the Discalced ("barefoot") Carmelites, who followed a far stricter rule than their shod sisters. Teresa wrote books and letters that established her as one of the great mystics of all times. A clear-headed, charming, intelligent, and spiritual woman, she blended an active life with one of deep contemplation. She died in 1582, was canonized forty years later, and was proclaimed a Doctor of the Church in 1970—the first woman to be so honored. Her day is October 15.

Santa Teresa is patron of Spain, of Spanish Catholic writers, of the Commisariat of the Spanish army, and of faith. She is depicted wearing a nun's habit, which usually is black and white. She also may hold a crucifix, a crosier, and a banner on which are inscribed the letters "IHS," the first three letters of "Jesus" in the Greek alphabet and thus Christ's monogram. She sometimes wears a medal bearing the same legend, or may be shown writing in a book. She is invoked against headaches and heart disease.

SAINT TERESA OF AVILA

OPPOSITE: *This Spanish colonial painting of Santa Teresa was made in Mexico by an unknown artist and then brought to Santa Fe, New Mexico, where it now occupies a place in the altar screen of the San Miguel chapel. It dates from the late seventeenth or early eighteen centuries.*

ACKNOWLEDGMENTS

MANY PEOPLE HAVE HELPED in this project. In southern Arizona, I received invaluable aid from Father Alberic Smith, O.F.M., and John Vidal of Mission San Xavier del Bac, and Vernon Barney, Kristine Cobb, Don Garate, Steve Gastellum and Ray Madril of Tumacácori National Historical Park. Also, Father Daniel McLaughlin, S.T., of Blessed Kateri Tekakwitha Parish allowed me to photograph in the chapel at Saint Nicholas Indian Center. The owners and staff of the Little Mexico Restaurant in Tucson served me wonderful food and let us photograph their shrine to San Martín Caballero. Elaine Mariel also helped in that project. Finally, the Armando González family generously allowed me to photograph their San Judas chapel.

In Sonora, Licenciado Francisco Manzo Taylor of Hermosillo proved to be an excellent and knowledgeable guide, as well as a fount of ideas and information concerning his beloved home state. R.P. Guillermo Coronado of San Miguel de Ures and R.P. Priciliano Celaya of San Miguel Horcasitas graciously permitted me to photograph in the churches under their care.

In Chihuahua, Sandra Casillas of Casas Grandes provided excellent leads, as did numerous residents of Mata Ortiz, past and present. In particular, Gaby Domínguez and Blanca Ponce escorted us to a

Ramona López of the pottery-making community of Mata Ortiz, Chihuahua, with her print of San Ysidro. Señora López holds a fiesta in honor of San Ysidro every year on his day.

wonderful Guadalupe shrine, Lilia Belo permitted us to photograph her Santa Niño capilla, and Ramona López showed us her great-grandmother's San Ysidro picture.

In New Mexico, Charlie Carrillo and Father Thomas J. Steele, S.J., provided important leads and perspectives. Charlie and his parents, Ralph and Loretta Carrillo, also opened their homes to us and to our cameras and questions. Manny and Sophia Gurulé of Santa Fe and Eulogio and Zoraida Ortega of Velarde graciously permitted us to visit and photograph in their private chapels. The owners and employees of the P and C Restaurant and Castro's Mexican Food Restaurant also served great meals and allowed us to get in their way with our camera equipment.

We are indebted to the Most Reverend Archbishop Michael J. Sheehan of the Archdiocese of Santa Fe for permission to photograph in the churches of his archdiocese, and to the Reverend Ron Carrillo, the Reverend Adán Ortega, and the Reverend Miguel Mateo for welcoming us into their respective churches. We also are indebted to many other people—whose names we never learned—who smoothed the way for us everywhere we went.

Finally, I want to thank Ross Humphreys, whom I discovered is an even better traveling companion than he is a photographer—and that's saying a lot!